WITHDRAWN

What Does "Queer" Mean Anyway?

The Quick and Dirty Guide to LGBTQIA+ Vocabulary

Chris Bartlett

Chris Bartlett

Copyright © 2016 by It's the Journey Not The Destination LLC

All rights reserved. This book or any portion thereof may not be reproduced or used in any manner whatsoever without the express written permission of the publisher except for the use of brief quotations in a book review.

Printed in the United States of

America First Printing, 2016

It's the Journey not the Destination LLC
PO Box 350457

Westminster CO 80035-0457
www.thequickanddirtyguide.com

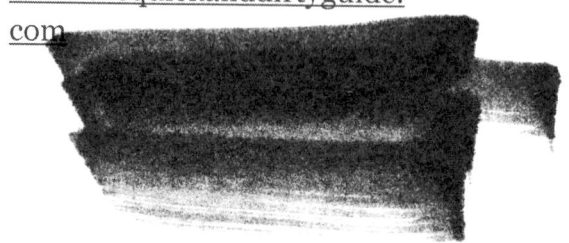

What Does "Queer" Mean Anyway?

From the Author

Several years ago a gay friend of mine called me an "ally." It was flattering, but I quickly began to feel guilty. I don't think I ever deliberately demeaned anyone on the LGBTQIA+ spectrum — but not hurting others is hardly a heroic act. In fact, when I was younger I was a regular church attendee and when put on the spot I would claim to hold the same conservative views regarding alternative lifestyles that my church and family held. These words were at odds with my having an increasing number of friends who were publicly or privately of an alternative orientation or gender identity (terms that will be explained in the following text); eventually I stopped affirming these views – but I also did not say anything else on the topic.

As I have grown older and hopefully wiser I have come to realize that not even my past silence on homophobia and transphobia was not harmless. Following the homophobia-inspired massacre in Orlando on June 11th, 2016 I have searched my memories for every moment I didn't speak out against hate or tacitly agreed with it through my silence. I will never really know if

Chris Bartlett

I gave cover to someone who might one day develop malicious intent.

I began this book before the murders in Orlando, so I cannot claim that it is a response to those events. Neither will I say that it is a penance for past actions; at least, it isn't *only* that. Rather, it is a product of my belief that people want to be good to their fellows and it is most often fear and ignorance that prevent us from doing so. Most people have no desire to be hurtful or discriminatory towards those of alternative identities, but often feel at a loss for how to understand and approach them on equitable terms. Many Americans are just recently finding themselves comfortable with homosexuality and are surprised to discover that there are more identities that they now need to account for. Many more are still acclimating to "sex" and "gender" not meaning the same things (if that describes you, never fear, the difference is explained in this book.)

This book is written for them; for those who are curious, well meaning, but perhaps not completely comfortable with people who identify in ways that our culture has traditionally not accepted. This book is non-confrontational and non-judgmental; come as you are and leave as

What Does "Queer" Mean Anyway?

you will.

Thank you,
Chris

Chris Bartlett

Table of Contents

Introduction	VII
Chapter 1: What Is LGBTQIA+?	1
Chapter 2: Transgender And Intersex	11
Chapter 3: Gender Fluidity And Nonconformity	22
Chapter 4: Tackling Judgment And Prejudice	30
Chapter 5: Relationships In Which Only One Person Is Transgender	37
Chapter: Gender Identity, Sexuality, And Popular Culture	44
Conclusion	50
To My Friends In The LGBTQIA+ Community	53
Bibliography	55
I Need Your Help	59
Stay Informed About My Next Project!	60

What Does "Queer" Mean Anyway?

Introduction

In the United States, 3.5% of adults formally identify as lesbian, gay or bisexual and 0.3% are transgender. Intersex makes up 1.7%. This tells us that over 9 million Americans are officially under the LGBTQIA+ umbrella. However, this only accounts for those who have declared their sexuality or gender identity for public records and are publicly sure of their personal identity description. There are likely to be significantly more people who would identify as LGBTQIA+ if it weren't for social, religious, or cultural factors discouraging them. Not only that, but as both sexuality and gender belong on a spectrum rather than in separate boxes and categories, there are many people who may fall somewhere in the grey zone between identities. For example, 8% of Americans state that they have experienced a same-sex intimate encounter, and 11% acknowledge some sort of same sex attraction, but that does not necessarily mean these people are categorized as gay or bisexual (Gates 2011). When it comes to gender, increasing numbers of people are identifying as gender neutral, nonbinary, or two-spirit, with modern culture presenting us with a rainbow tapestry of terminology and descriptions.

The worldwide figures on LGBTQIA+ populations are not possible to measure. As of 2016, 77 countries still uphold laws that make much of what the LGBTQIA+ acronym signifies illegal and punishable. Many billions of people are also committed to religions that traditionally condemn behaviors that are natural and healthy to those who identify one way or another under this umbrella acronym. It is unlikely that correct data about LGBTQIA+ representation can be collected from such demographics. Regardless of these impediments, however, the global movement for recognition is marching forward and it is important that the surrounding issues be understood.

The purpose of this book is to simplify complicated and ever-evolving concepts of gender identities and sexual orientations. It includes personal case studies which attempt to outline the deeply intricate issues that arise from belonging to a sexual or gender minority, as well as larger societal implications and interactions. The book also aims to eliminate myths and stereotypes, with a focus on factual

What Does "Queer" Mean Anyway?

information and unpacking common terms and phrases used in everyday conversation when talking about gender and sexuality. Whether you are close with a member of the LGBTQIA+ community or not, this book should shed light on a wide range of topics.

As a final note, remember that the terms used in this book are not static. Some words that were acceptable in 2000 are now considered distasteful, and other words that were originally meant to be discriminatory have been reclaimed by members of the LGBTQIA+ community who use them with pride. The best way to find out how someone identifies is to respectfully ask them — and, of course, honor their wishes.

What Does "Queer" Mean Anyway?

Chapter 1: What Is LGBTQIA+?

Most readers have probably heard or seen the acronym LGBT and are aware it stands for Lesbian, Gay, Bisexual, Transgender (although they may mistakenly believe the "T" is for "Transexual"). The Q, I, and A additions are less familiar to mainstream audiences, but they will be explained below. Some variation of the acronym is used in everyday language and appears regularly in mainstream media, workplaces, and public literature. Regardless of the form, it is used to collectively describe communities of people whose sexual identity differs from the historically accepted heterosexual (straight) identity or whose gender differs from the cisgendered male and female definitions. (Cisgendered will be explained below as well.) In this book we will continue to use the acronym in full but that is not to imply that it cannot be shortened or that the entire acronym has to be spelled out each time it is referred to.

Looking at each of the letters in LGBTQIA+ can be helpful for better understanding its meaning, but first we should get on the same page with some other vocabulary. Throughout this book sexual orientations and genders will sometimes be compared to heterosexuality and cisgendered identities. This is not meant to imply that those identities are more normal or in anyway superior to the ones on the LGBTQIA+ spectrum, though they are probably more familiar to the bulk of the readership.

Heterosexuality: This orientation applies to people who identify as one gender but are attracted to the opposite. Often referred to as "straight."

Cisgendered (abbreviated to **cis):** a term for people whose gender identity matches their assigned (birth) sex. An individual can be described as a cis man or a cis woman.

Male bodied: This refers to an individual with male sexual organs, regardless of their sex at birth; i.e., someone who has a penis and testicles.

Female bodied: This refers to an individual with female sexual organs, regardless of their sex at birth; i.e., someone who has a vagina, breasts, a uterus, etc.

What Does "Queer" Mean Anyway?

Now, onto the **LGBTQIA+** acronym:

L stands for Lesbian. A lesbian is a female (or someone who identifies as a female) who is sexually attracted to other females.

G stands for Gay. A gay person is, in this context, a male (or someone who identifies as male) who is sexually attracted to other males. "Gay" can also refer to a female who is attracted to other females but who would prefer to be described this way rather than as a "lesbian."

B stands for Bisexual (abbreviated to Bi). This refers to a person who has the potential to be sexually attracted to more than one gender.

T stands for Transgender. A transgender person is someone whose gender identity does not match their biological (sometimes called their "assigned") sex. It refers to someone who feels they are living in a body that does not match their inner gender identity, whether or not they plan to surgically transition. Some may assume that this "T" stands for "Transsexual," but that term is used with decreasing frequency and is often considered offensive. Still others may think that this "T" has something to do with "Transvestitism," but that is not always true — and a topic for a completely different book.

Chris Bartlett

Q stands for Queer. In the past this word was used derisively for people of a non-heterosexual or non-cisgendered identity. When the gay rights movement gained strength in the 1990s and early 2000s the younger generation of activists popularized the word being used positively. (Chevez, 2010) It has now been largely appropriated by people who feel their sexual and/or gender identify is fluid and either shifts from time to time or is simply inadequately described by other definitions. It is also used as a general term for people who identify somewhere on the LGBTQIA+ spectrum, in effect an abbreviation of an acronym. The phrase "Queer Community" is also used as an umbrella term for people on who identify within the spectrum.

Lola is a 31 year old female, divorced from an eight year marriage. After their (Lola's) divorce, they were confused about their sexual and gender identity. They had always been attracted to women, and they were still attracted to some men, but not very masculine men. They also noticed their attraction and their own gender presentation and identity shifting over time. They saw themselves as neither a man nor a woman, and did not want to be constrained by society's definitions of such. Because their gender and sexuality often

What Does "Queer" Mean Anyway?

shifted and could not be explained in a tidy definition or common phrase, they chose to call themselves a queer genderqueer, and they began to use neutral pronouns.

I stands for Intersex. An intersex person has unique anatomical or chromosomal structures, which means they physically do not fit into either a "fully male" or "fully female" identity. Intersexuality can be very subtle, or very obvious, depending on the characteristics of the individual's biology. For example, an intersex person may have outward male organs, but very little facial hair and semi- developed ovaries. More and more is always being learned about intersexuality, which is now better understood by healthcare professionals and the general public than it has been in the past. It can often lead to the need for corrective surgery or gender reassignment depending on the individual needs of the person. It may interest you to know that one of the first trans-women to have gender-reassignment surgery, Lili Elbe (whose life was portrayed in the 2015 film *The Danish Girl*), was actually intersex, a concept that would not have been well understood when she was alive in the 1930s (Meyerowitz 2002).

A stands for Asexual. An asexual person may be of any physical or gender identity but does not experience sexual attraction.

At times a "+" sign is included in the acronym to indicate that its current form is not necessarily all-inclusive. This sign's inclusion in the acronym can be read as an encouragement for those who do not find themselves fitting into any of the other groups, yet also do not identify as heterosexual or cisgendered, to feel supported in their exploration and self-identification.

Some people wonder why these definitions are all grouped together under one umbrella. After all, a person's sexuality doesn't necessarily have any impact on their gender whatsoever, and vice versa. The two areas can be essentially separate, and although there can sometimes be some overlap between gender and sexuality, many gay rights activists and transgender activists are calling for a formal acknowledgement of their separate meanings.

When a person does want to change their biological sex, for example if they were born male bodied and want to be female bodied, then gender affirmation surgery (also called reassignment surgery and sometimes known as a sex change) as well

What Does "Queer" Mean Anyway?

as a complex set of procedures including hormone treatments are options. Access to these very much depends on the country the person is living in and the laws that apply there. However, when a person does change gender, or begins living as another gender, it can have an impact on the language used to describe their sexual identity and orientation. Here's a case study to consider:

Jane was born a male called John but now lives as a woman. She has had a number of hormonal treatments to make her breast tissue grow. She is awaiting a full sex change operation to remove her male sexual organs but has to undertake counseling first. She always felt different as a male child and that she didn't belong in a male body. As she grew up, Jane knew she was sexually attracted to females and was therefore considered to be a heterosexual (straight) young man. Once Jane realized she wanted to live as a woman, as this would reflect her inner identity, she began dressing in women's clothes and changed her name from John to Jane. During her process, some family and friends assumed that Jane was a gay man having identity issues. In fact, Jane remained attracted to women throughout her transformation, meaning that by the time she transitioned to being a woman she was technically a lesbian.

With this case study in mind, some might argue that the interaction between gender and sexuality give good reason for the LGBTQIA+ acronym to remain as it is.

More complicated language can arise when gender and sexuality are not so cut and dry. There exist a few other concepts that do not get a direct mention in the LGBTQIA+ acronym but still land under the umbrella.

Pansexual: A person who considers themselves to be pansexual is not limited by gender definitions or biological sex. They are attracted to an individual regardless of how that person identifies.

Nonbinary: A nonbinary person does not adhere to the traditional categories of man or woman but can dress, behave, and appear to be male, female, both, or neither. This is synonymous with "genderqueer."

Gender Fluid: A gender-fluid person expresses a range of genders that can evolve or change over time, from male and female to non-binary.

Two-Spirit: Originally a term used by some

What Does "Queer" Mean Anyway?

of the indigenous people of North America, this refers to people who feel their body hosts both a masculine and a feminine spirit, therefore celebrating both genders simultaneously.

Here's another case study to better understand some of these terms:

Rachael is a 24-year-old cis woman. She identifies as pansexual and enjoys activities and hobbies such as cycling, drawing, and archery. A woman called Jo has recently joined her archery team. Jo is also 24 but doesn't look "typically" female. She has shaved hair, wears casual shirts and ties, but also wears a full face of makeup. Jo identifies as a gender-fluid lesbian. Sometimes Jo wears dresses and skirts and behaves in a very stereotypical feminine manner, whereas other days she prefers a more butch and masculine appearance. Rachael is attracted to Jo, and the two of them begin dating. Many people assume Rachael is a lesbian, but to Rachael, Jo's gender or sex is not a factor in her attraction. Many also assume that Jo is likely to one day transition into a male, or is confused about her gender, when in fact is she quite comfortable displaying her gender in a fluid and nonbinary way.

The above case study helps us to understand that there are many, many blends of definitions and language when it comes to gender, sex, and sexuality.

This chapter was aimed at distinguishing between sexuality and gender. The following chapters will investigate gender identity further.

What Does "Queer" Mean Anyway?

Chapter 2: Transgender and Intersex

This chapter aims to differentiate between a transgender person and an intersex person. It also looks at surrounding sociological factors and how transgenderism and intersexuality come about in the first place.

An intersex person is born with ambiguous anatomy that does not necessarily adhere to one specific sex. It is estimated that up to 1.7% of births are intersexed (Women's Resource Centre 2016).

Traditionally, the parents of a baby known to be intersex have been encouraged to choose a sex for their child at birth; however, in more recent times, doctors recommend a more gender- neutral upbringing to allow the intersex person to find their own identity.

Intersexuality can be divided into four categories. These are called "46, XX intersex," "46, XY intersex," "true gonadal intersex," and "complex or undetermined intersex" (Kaneshiro 2015). These categories all sound very complicated, especially to those without a background in biology. However, they can be explained in pretty basic terms.

46, XX Intersex

A person who is 46, XX intersex has female chromosomes, ovaries, and a generally female "inside," but external male genitals; this can be caused by a female fetus being exposed to excessive amounts of male hormones before birth. A deformity of the labia and clitoris causes an enlargement that looks like a penis. A famous case of a 46, XX Intersex person is Britain's Lady Colin Campbell, who through much of her childhood was mistaken for a boy and had to undergo surgeries and transformation to become her true sex.

46, XY Intersex

A person who is 46, XY intersex has male chromosomes but external genitals that are incomplete or ambiguous. Testes may be completely normal, malformed or non-existent due to an imbalance in male and female hormones.

True Gonadal Intersex

This person has both ovarian and testicular tissue. Genitals are likely to be ambiguous and the underlying cause is

What Does "Queer" Mean Anyway?

unknown.

Complex or Undetermined Intersex

As the name suggests, people who fall into this category of intersexuality have chromosome configurations other than 46, XX or 46, XY. It can have serious consequences resulting in disorders of sex development and is far more complex than other categories.

There are a range of symptoms that point to someone being intersex. Usually these are apparent at birth and can be recognized quickly. In other situations, these symptoms do not present until puberty. In fact, a delay in reaching puberty is a common sign that requires investigation for signs of intersexuality (Kaneshiro 2015).

It is important for intersex people to get a diagnosis even if it is at a late stage. Physical differences sometimes do not affect an intersex person's life dramatically. In other circumstances the news can be traumatic. The below case study shows how the news can be both a welcome relief and also a life changing shock:

Linda was born outwardly female. She spent her childhood looking and feeling female with no signs of gender or sex ambiguity. She had a normal, functional social group and excelled at school. When Linda reached 15, most of her friends were menstruating and had growing breast tissue. Linda became embarrassed about her flat chest and would wear a bra stuffed with toilet tissue to give the illusion of breasts instead. She would skip gym lessons, stating she had migraines. She even convinced her doctor of these pretend migraines to get a sick note in order to miss anything that involved changing into her gym clothes. She did not go to sleepovers and was increasingly isolated. When her ever-shrinking circle of friends asked her about her periods, she would avoid the subject. By age 17 Linda's mother took her to a doctor to discuss the situation. She was referred to a specialist, and after several tests and scans, Linda was told she was intersex and had no ovaries. The news was shocking at first, as Linda had never even heard of this condition before. But she felt relieved that there was an explanation for the differences she experienced. As the news sunk in, Linda realized that, in the future, having children would be complicated, but she was grateful to learn about this news at a young age, which maximized her chances of living a happy life, whatever her sex or gender identity.

What Does "Queer" Mean Anyway?

In some cases, a person is in their mid-to-late life before acknowledging that something is different and seeking answers about their internal and external anatomy. For an older person this can often be traumatic if they see and experience more stigmatization in gender identity issues from their peers of the same age.

Intersexuality is still very misunderstood in many countries, but with a slow progression of science-based evidence, and a general understanding of the biology and psychology involved, intersex people can live fairer and more fulfilled lives.

The next section of this chapter looks at Transgenderism. Before moving on, it's important to reiterate the difference between sex and gender.

Sex is primarily concerned with physical attributes like hormones and internal and external sex organs. Gender refers to the socially constructed roles, characteristics and behaviors that are typical of being either a man or a woman (American Psychological Association 2015).

Many identities fall under the transgender umbrella and one of these is the term "transgendered." This refers to people who feel that their gender identity is different from their birth sex. In many cases this can lead to body alteration, hormonal treatment, or gender reassignment surgery. Another term for reassignment surgery is "gender affirmation."

If a person is born female, but identifies and lives as man — with or without medical intervention — they would be referred to as a trans man or female-to-male (FTM). Similarly, a person who was born male but identifies and lives as a woman would be referred to as a trans woman or male-to-female (MTF).

While it is not certain whether there are biological causes for transgenderism, some significant schools of thought strongly suggest neurobiological origins. This means that something happens in-utero that might change or alter the development of the unborn child's central nervous system. According to recent findings, certain brain tissue differences have been correlated with apparent cross-gender body feelings and mixed self-perceptions (Conway 2003).

Another biomedical cause could have to do with the brain structure of transgender people. A team at the National University of Distance Education in Madrid, led by scientist Antonio Guillamon, believes they

What Does "Queer" Mean Anyway?

have evidence that certain structures of brain matter in female-to-male transgender people resemble those typically found in the male brain, and those of male-to-female transgender people do not (Hamzelou 2011).

Other theories attribute transgenderism to traumatic childhood events, or an underlying mental health condition, though none of these can be definitively proven or disproven.

You may have heard of the term "gender dysphoria." This is becoming a regularly used term in medicine and popular culture. Gender dysphoria is a psychological condition in which a person feels discomfort, unhappiness, or extreme distress due to a perceived mismatch between their biological sex and gender identity. It is not necessarily a cause of transgenderism, but rather a psychological symptom of being in the "wrong body." However, in many cases, the diagnosis of this condition can open up doorways to treatments, surgeries and counseling to help an individual make choices about their gender identity. In many western countries, a diagnosis of gender dysphoria must be agreed upon by two or more specialists following an in-depth assessment. From this assessment, relevant action can be taken if required (NHS.uk 2016).

Regardless of the "cause" of transgenderism, it exists in every society, in every country in the world, and has done so throughout history. When we look back through history books, we can see transgenderism being displayed as early as 1503 BC, when the Egyptian Queen Hatshepsut ascended to the throne and adopted a masculine persona to rule. The timeline of transgender history shows significant progress around the 1920s to 1950s when some of the first transgender operations in history were pioneered, and hormone intervention was introduced (cbc.ca 2016). The road has been rocky, with many milestones achieved through the help and influence of popular culture, music, theater, political activists, and, of course, the medical community.

A modern approach to helping transgender people form their preferred gender identity is to begin the transition (if one is needed and wanted) as early as possible. You have likely heard in recent times about transgender children. This can be a controversial topic. However, guidelines given by The World Professional Association for Transgender Health state

What Does "Queer" Mean Anyway?

that a pre-puberty social transition with support from mental health experts is the first step to allowing a child manifest their gender identity. Experts are sensitive to the differences between transgenderism and gender non-conformity, and welcome a person-centered approach to "treating" the individual. Physical intervention may become available in adolescence. These can be a desirable option to prevent certain unwelcome hormonal changes from occurring which could cause psychological distress to the transgender child; for example, if a child wants to transition to male, it is unlikely that growing a pair of breasts at puberty will positively impact the child and therefore hormones can be given to stop this process. Some interventions are fully reversible in case there is a decision to revert back to the child's original sex. (Coleman et al 2012).

The following case study gives an example of how, by not transitioning early, transgenderism can be a difficult process for someone who is already in established adulthood.

Robert is a 65-year-old widower. He is active in his community and a local church member. Many of his friends have known him for at least 30 years, and he has lived in the same house for that period of time.

Chris Bartlett

He has three sons who are all married and live locally. Robert has always felt different, and from an early age was cross-dressing. His father caught him trying on his mother's clothes as a child and harshly punished him. While he was married, Robert had fantasies about being able to do the same activities as his wife, such as shopping for women's shoes, attending women's book clubs, and trying on lipsticks at the local makeup counter. When his wife passed away from cancer, Robert grieved for several years, but his community and sons kept him going. Over time, he allowed his instincts to take over and began to cross-dress in private. After three years of secretly being a woman called Tabby at home, Robert decided to slowly introduce Tabby to the outside world. This involved the difficult ordeal of having to tell his sons, who were confused, embarrassed, and angry. As Robert emerged less and less, Tabby moved to the forefront. Tabby began to go to the shops, social events, and local clubs as her preferred identity. Unfortunately, many people in her existing social groups abandoned her, and Tabby received a letter from the church leader suggesting she undergo some psychological help before returning to future Sunday services and that returning to the church

What Does "Queer" Mean Anyway?

meant returning as Robert. Tabby still looked very male, with facial stubble and masculine features, and felt stared at and judged. After a year of living fully as Tabby, she was given the all clear by her doctor for beginning a process of transitioning physically. This was a difficult, painful process, which two of her three sons could not agree with. With the support of a local trans group and one of her sons, however, Tabby regained some control over her life and underwent a variety of surgeries, including gender affirmation surgery (also called "gender reassignment surgery"). She realized she would need to start from scratch in many ways, as a new person, and often wondered if her life would have been easier if she had done something about her identity at a younger age.

Chris Bartlett

Chapter 3: Gender Fluidity and Nonconformity

In the above chapters, we looked at the differences between sexuality and gender, as well as a more detailed view of intersexuality and transgenderism.

This chapter will look at gender fluidity and nonconformist gender identities such as "non- binary" and "gender neutral."

Gender is taught to us from the moment we are born. It is a social construct and is not determined solely by sex but rather as how a culture has reacted to sexual differences. Some of these reactions may be relatively benign, such as it being considered polite for men to open doors for women. Other reactions may be tantamount to slavery; like the now-extinct Chinese tradition of foot binding or women not being permitted to vote in the United States until the early 20th century.

Think for a moment about the way boys and girls are treated according to their

What Does "Queer" Mean Anyway?

perceived gender as children. Boys from a young age wear colors like blue, brown and orange, have haircuts to keep their hair short, play with toy trucks and tool sets, and dress up as action heroes. Even the language printed on western boys' and girls' clothing is different. Boys wear t-shirts with words like "monster," "brave," "King," "surfer-dude," "cool," "biker," etc. Girl's clothes often have words like "princess," "cutie," "adorable," "daddy's-girl," "little lady," etc. This treatment continues as we grow up. Boys are persuaded to engage in certain competitive team sports, watch "guy films," and be chivalrous towards women. Girls are encouraged to get involved in more graceful sports like horseback riding or gymnastics, watch "chick-flicks," and conduct themselves in a subdued, ladylike, sheltered way. Of course these activities evolve through different eras, and in more recent times these roles and hobbies are blending between genders, allowing for a more open arena of interests and behaviors.

Another consideration is that due to the socio- political imbalance between sexes, women's gender has been constructed by men, or as a man's ideal image of women. Laura Mulvey, scholarly author of Visual Pleasure and Narrative Cinema, wisely observed:

Chris Bartlett

"In a world ordered by sexual imbalance, pleasure in looking has been split between active/male and passive/female. The determining male gaze projects its fantasy onto the female figure, which is styled accordingly." What this means is that while it may come across as "natural" to have a particular feminine style, this style has been an evolving construct created by men to fulfill their own sexual fantasy. Is femininity just a way of attracting men? If a woman were to become stuck, alone, on a desert island and could only take limited items with her, would lipstick and a push-up bra really be considered important?

The association of certain colors with different genders began in the early 20th century. In 1927, *Time* magazine printed a chart of pioneering gender-appropriate color- schemes for girls and boys (Wolchover 2012). At this time pink was actually assigned to boys, and blue to girls. Pink was considered a stronger and more masculine color, whereas blue was more dainty and passive. These color connotations are reflective of attitudes towards gender that existed at the time. A mix of marketing ploys and contemporary literature slowly swapped these colors around, and they are still prominent today.

What Does "Queer" Mean Anyway?

Another artificial construction is society's reaction to crying. While crying in public is often considered embarrassing for both sexes, the average woman tends to receive less scrutiny for why she was crying than would a man who is shedding tears. This is in contrast to the ways that many cultures tolerated or even encouraged men displaying emotions in the past. Ancient Greek stories are replete with male protagonists weeping, even in response to an emotional song. The Old Testament includes many references to Ancient Hebrews crying; the authors of the Gospels were not bothered by directly saying that "Jesus wept." Yet today many young boys are admonished for crying, and when difficulties are experiences they are encouraged to "take it like a man." (Lutz 2001)

One way of gaining a simple overview into gender is to consider it as a spectrum. At each end of the spectrum is a "man" and "woman," with a number of stop-offs in between. Gender fluidity means that a person may travel freely along this spectrum, whereas a gender neutral or gender nonconformist person may not slide along the scale freely but be firmly planted somewhere between the two ends. This might mean landing close to the "man" end in most ways but feeling quite feminine and behaving in mildly feminine ways (as defined by society), or it could mean being nearer the "woman" end in many respects but still having certain traits and behaviors that are typically male.

So how do we refer to someone if they are gender neutral or nonconformist? It may not always be appropriate to use the pronouns "he" or "she," so what other options are there?

1. They used singularly
2. Ne (pronounced like "knee")
3. Ve (pronounced like "V")
4. Ey (pronounced like "A")
5. Ze (pronounced like "Z")
6. Xe (also pronounced like "Z")

The following table can show you exactly how to use these in context when talking to or about a gender neutral person. There is no standard on how to use these pronouns or which orientation uses which variation. Normally individuals select which pronouns they prefer. Because of this it is more appropriate to ask someone if they have a pronoun preference that

What Does "Queer" Mean Anyway?

differs from the mainstream and attempt to respect it. Most people are aware that others have been using traditional pronouns all of their lives and will not react negatively to accidental misusage.

Pronouns	Subject pronouns	Object pronouns	Possessive determiner	Possessive Pronouns	Reflexive Pronouns
He	He ran	I followed	His hair is red	That is his	He likes himself

She	She ran	I followed her	Her hair is red	That is hers	She likes herself
They	They ran	I followed them	Their hair is red	That is theirs	They like themself
Ne	Ne ran	I followed nem	Nir hair is red	That is nirs	Ne likes nemself

Chris Bartlett

Ve	Ve ran	I followed ver	Vis hair is red	That is vis	Ve likes verself
Ey	Ey ran	I followed em	Eir hair is red	That is eirs	Ey likes emself
Ze and hir	Ze ran	I followed hir	Hir hair is red	That is hirs	Ze likes hirself
Ze and zir	Ze ran	I followed zir	Zir hair is red	That is zirs	Ze likes zirself
Xe	Xe ran	I called xem	Xyr hair is red	That is xyrs	Xe likes xemsel

So let's use some of these in sentences to extend our familiarity:

Zoe loves cakes. Ne prefers lemon drizzle to Bakewell tarts. Nir least favorite is a fruit cake.

Wilson thought to xemself that it was better to arrive at the theater with xyr friends early than be late.

Rebecca couldn't believe the state of eir hair. Ey couldn't wait to see a hairdresser.

What Does "Queer" Mean Anyway?

There is not necessarily a "proper" pronoun to use when discussing any type of individual. In time a societal consensus may coalesce around which pronouns are most applicable to which individual, but for now allowing an individual the choice and a voice in how to be referred to is the best option.

Gender Nonconformity in Children

Gender nonconformity can emerge naturally in children from a young age. Many children experiment with gender roles in childhood without it having any impact on the rest of their lives. A 2012 study conducted by the Children's Hospital Of Chicago demonstrated the advantages of affirming a child's right to be gender neutral, gender variant, or gender nonconforming. It suggested that there is a difference between affirming a gender identity and encouraging it. According to the study, affirming can lead to a decreased risk of disruptive adolescence and higher self-esteem (Garofalo 2012).

Chapter 4: Tackling Judgment and Prejudice

While many countries around the world are embracing LGBTQIA+ culture, encouraging global discussion on implementing a fairer society, there are some countries and cultures that are still very much opposed to anything that relates to being gay, gender nonconformist, or transgender.

Often LGBTQIA+ people are discriminated against, penalized, judged, or even attacked due to their orientation or gender identity. This is often referred to as "homophobia," as "biphobia," or as "transphobia." Let's look at these terms in more detail:

Homophobia: This is fear or hatred of homosexuals which can be expressed directly or indirectly towards the person. It can include hostility, unfair treatment, or making cruel jokes and remarks.
Biphobia: This is the fear or hatred of bisexual people, which can, again, be expressed directly or indirectly and involve many types of cruelty, unfair treatment, or hostility. A similar

What Does "Queer" Mean Anyway?

phenomenon is known as "bi-erasure." This is when a person who self-identifies as bisexual is regarded as being either homosexual or heterosexual. A prominent example of bi-erasure can be found in a popular impression of the late Freddie Mercury, the lead singer of the rock band Queen. Although he is known to have had a long-running intimate relationship with a woman, he is frequently remembered as a gay man.

Transphobia: This is the fear or hatred of transgender people, which can include teasing, belittling, disregarding, making jokes about their gender, or acting hostile or threatening violence.

Unfortunately, for LGBTQIA+ communities, how they can expect to be treated and received by others is very much a location lottery. For example, in 2001, The Netherlands became the first country in the world to legalize same-sex marriage. The Netherlands has been, and continues to be, a liberal and free country where an LGBTQIA+ person or couple should expect to experience only limited amounts of homophobia or transphobia. Their marriage equality law was closely followed by others in Belgium and Canada in 2003, Spain in 2005, South Africa in 2006, Norway in 2009, the United Kingdom in 2013, and the United States in

Chris Bartlett

2015 (Procon.org 2014).

In contrast, LGBTQIA+ communities face prosecution and social persecution in many other countries around the world. In Morocco, Bangladesh, Pakistan, Jamaica, and Singapore there are still laws criminalizing homosexuality and transgenderism.

These identities are currently considered activities that are punishable by prison, and in some cases, death. Implementation of such laws is frequently inconsistent and in some cases very rare, depending upon the country.

With homosexuality and transgenderism still being illegal or forbidden in so many densely populated countries around the world, LGBTQIA+ communities are pushed underground, and those in them forced to keep their relationships and identities a secret. This also limits their access to basic healthcare, as fear of arrest or persecution can deter many LGBTQIA+ people from asking for condoms and other contraceptives. This shaded view of sexuality and gender can put a person's mental and physical health at risk. Even in areas where LGBTQIA+ groups are progressing

What Does "Queer" Mean Anyway?

towards full equality, such as in the United Kingdom and the United States, there is still an ongoing effort to ensure that the treatment of these communities is fair and responsible. Language plays a big part in this. The following words and phrases are considered unacceptable and should be avoided when talking to or about an LGBTQIA+ person. Please note that this is not an exhaustive list.

Dyke – An offensive word meaning "lesbian." Recently there have been trends toward reclaiming this word (like "queer"), but it should not be used to describe a person without express permission.
Poof – An offensive word meaning "gay."
Faggot – An offensive word referring to either a gay man or gay woman/lesbian.
Fairy – Often used offensively to describe a feminine or gender-nonconforming male or gay man.
Nancy – An offensive way to describe a gay man, or man with feminine or gender nonconforming traits or behaviors. **Sexual Preference** – This is a common mistake — the correct term should be "sexual orientation" or "sexuality." "Sexual preference" implies a person's sexual identity is a matter of choice.
Sodomite – This is an old fashioned and very offensive term used to describe

a gay man.

Gay Sex – The correct term is "sex." There is no need for the word "gay" as a modifier.

Tranny - An offensive term used to describe a transgender person.

Gay Lifestyle – This is an offensive term which implies that being gay is a lifestyle choice.

She-Male – An offensive term used to describe transgender or gender nonconformist people.

It is also important to understand the way everyday prejudices, judgments, assumptions, and direct or indirect discrimination can impact on the life of an LGBTQIA+ person.

The following two case studies give an illustration of this:

Mohammed is 18 and identifies as gay and a gender-queer male. He has a boyfriend, Joel, whom he loves. Mohammed and Joel take a short vacation to France for their first anniversary. When they check into the hotel, the porter refers to Mohammed as "Madam." Mohammed jokes about this nervously at the front desk. He isn't sure if the porter was joking, mistaken, or mocking him. When they check into their

What Does "Queer" Mean Anyway?

room, they notice they've been given separate single beds. Joel goes to the front desk to rearrange a room with a double bed, but the manager says they are fully booked. The next morning, Joel and Mohammed are walking through the hotel when they notice that many rooms are unoccupied. They choose to leave the hotel and find another so that they can be together at night. This caused them extra hassle and costs.

Terry is a transgender man, and works as a shop assistant in Ireland. He starts a new job at a family-run shop. On his first day, he is shown around the building. He asks his new colleague to show him to the restroom. Terry is shown to a female bathroom. Terry feels embarrassed, and explains that he will need a male bathroom instead. After this, word gets out that Terry has used a male bathroom. The manager speaks to Terry in private and says that while they won't interfere with Terry's lifestyle choices, they would appreciate a more conservative and conformist approach at work. Terry quits his job and is left without employment.

These examples show us that, while gender and sexual identity are now better-understood concepts than ever before, with record-breaking general acceptance, there is still a long way to go in ensuring equality in all aspects of life.

Chapter 5: Relationships in Which Only One Person Is Transgender

To begin this chapter, think back to earlier when we met Robert, a 65-year-old widower who transitioned into Tabby following the death of his wife. Robert did not feel comfortable bringing Tabby to the forefront during the course of his marriage, and only felt the time was right when he became a widower. However, when Robert did eventually become Tabby, it put a strain on the family relationships, especially with two of her sons.

In some cases, transgender people decide to transition from their original sex while they are still married. In others, people transition before meeting their spouse and have to go through the process of explaining and reassuring them of the situation. A famous fictional example of this in UK popular culture, which at the time brought transgenderism into the limelight, was that of Hayley Cropper, a soap character on *Coronation Street* whose storyline made national headlines.

In the late 90's, Hayley disclosed to her on-stage boyfriend Roy that she was in fact a "pre-operative transgender male-to-female." The episodes that followed showed the struggle Roy went through to accept Hayley as Hayley, and not to focus on her past identity.

Whether a person is already in a relationship when they transition, or if they transition before embarking on a relationship, there is evidence that transition puts significant strain on overall relationship success, as it can cause the non- transitioning partner to question their own identity. A large-scale study conducted by the University Of Houston showed that only half of marriages and relationships succeed following gender reassignment, and of these the average length of the maintained relationship is five years (Colton-Meier et al, 2013).

So what happens when two people are in a marriage or serious relationship and one person wants to transition? Sometimes this decision can be a traumatic shock for the other partner, who may have been completely unaware of their spouse's true gender. In other situations, it can come as a relief — an answer as to why their partner has been unhappy. In either scenario, it is bound to stir feelings of loss, distance, and confusion, and no two couples are the same.

What Does "Queer" Mean Anyway?

In some situations, the remaining partner may dismiss the gender identity as a breakdown, mid-life crisis or a mental illness. In 2014, Dr. Paul R. McHugh, a high profile Professor of Psychiatry at Johns Hopkins University Hospital stated that transgenderism is a mental illness that is enabled by doctors who are willing to perform gender reassignment procedures (Mchugh 2014). Comments like this often encourage some couples to seek help from reparative therapy clinics, which aim to reverse the purported illusion of seeking a new gender identity. While many in the medical profession frown upon it, this is a path that some couples choose to explore as a first option.

Again, it is important to reiterate that gender and sexuality are not the same thing, but as we learned in Chapter 2, one can effect the other.

While the transitioning partner may feel they are becoming "themselves" for the first time, the couple still has challenges. They can either continue the relationship (as a same-sex relationship if it began as a hetero-relationship, or as a hetero-relationship if it began as a same-sex relationship), or they can end the relationship. This is a difficult situation that requires support to understand its complexities. Let's look at another case study to explore this situation further:

Winnie and Paul are a married couple in their 50s. They have no children and, while they are happy together, their marriage has always been rocky. Paul has always seemed dissatisfied, grumpy, and antisocial, making it hard for Winnie to include him in certain activities and holidays. They started couples counseling and Paul recently disclosed during a session that he felt female on the inside. He said he has always felt this way and has dressed in women's clothes and at times presented as a woman while Winnie was out. He said he enjoys when Winnie goes on holiday alone or with her girlfriends because he can sit at home all weekend as a female rather than a male. He said he is grumpy and antisocial because he doesn't feel his outer appearance reflects his inner identity. Winnie initially disregards this as a breakdown, and suggests Paul start seeing a professional to escape from these fantasies. Paul reluctantly agrees, as he can see how much this news has shaken his wife. After six months in couples counseling, Paul says it's impossible for him to live as he has any longer. He gives Winnie a choice: to either support him in

What Does "Queer" Mean Anyway?

transitioning, or leave him. He loves Winnie, but he can't stay with her as a man. Winnie decides to stay and see how she feels as time progresses. The journey is slow, often painful, and confusing, but as Paul transitions, Winnie realizes that the grumpy, antisocial man she once lived with is now a far happier, energetic, and good-humored woman called Pearl. She and Pearl begin their journey as friends. Winnie is unsure about how physically romantic she wants to be with Pearl because Winnie is not a lesbian, but with patience and support, the couple find their equilibrium.

Many people who have already transitioned and are on the hunt for a new partner at some stage discuss their pasts and the journeys that they have been on with those they become close to. It can be difficult to find someone who is comfortable with this situation. A transgender person is advised to communicate with their potential partners about where they are in their process and (if they wish) about their anatomy, providing reassurance and information as possible while expelling any myths. This sort of situation can be better explained by way of the following case study:

Chris Bartlett

Kyle is a 35-year-old transgender male. He was born female and transitioned at age 18. Kyle has had full sex reassignment, has a working penis, testicles, a beard, and has had full hormonal treatment to make his voice deeper. He has had a hysterectomy and looks very masculine. In his adult life, nobody has ever questioned his gender. Everyone he meets assumes he was born male. Kyle has chosen to keep his past private, even with casual partners. However, one day Kyle meets Rebecca, a local radiologist, and after dating for several months he falls in love with her. They have regular sex and spend lots of time together. Eventually, Rebecca expresses that she wants to move in together. Kyle sits Rebecca down and tells her that he'd like to share something with her. He explains he was born female, and that he didn't tell her because he didn't want to be judged or put her off him. At first Rebecca is furious that he kept this from her. She storms off and doesn't speak to Kyle for several days. However, she then realizes that Kyle is still Kyle, that his transition has not impacted on their relationship, and that after some learning she hopes to come to grips with the situation and continue her relationship with him.

What Does "Queer" Mean Anyway?

There may not be an easy way to talk about the issue of one's transgender identity with an existing spouse or future partner, but what is advised in all situations for optimal success is good communication, and to make use of the support available within the community to make the process as smooth as possible.

A note about the language used to describe relationships which involve bisexual people: When two people of the same sex are in a relationship it can be tempting to describe it as a "homosexual/gay/lesbian relationship." This is superficial and makes an assumption about the sexual orientations of the people involved. It is possible that one or both of the people involved are bisexual. It is best use the phrase "same-sex relationship" instead. The phrase "different-sex relationship" can be used for a relationship that many would assume involved two heterosexuals but actually involves at least one bisexual person. One other important phrase is "mixed-orientation relationship." This can describe a relationship where one member is bisexual and the other identifies differently.

Chris Bartlett

Chapter: Gender Identity, Sexuality, and Popular Culture

In previous chapters we have discussed the fact that gender is a social construct and a complicated spectrum with many blending elements. We have also looked briefly at history and how both gender and society have changed over the centuries, especially in more recent decades. We agree that it takes a series of influences to create a cultural norm, and that evolving these norms takes time.

The arts have had a huge influence over our perception of gender identity and sexuality. Over the past 50 years there have been many popular culture figures — musicians, activists, actors, directors, writers, and painters — all of whom have contributed to the development of the LGBTQIA+ landscape and expanded its boundaries.

The following timeline shows some key events, and figures hailed as pioneers over the century.

1930 Lili Elbe, Danish painter, has the

What Does "Queer" Mean Anyway?

first known gender reassignment surgery. Her life story is told in the 2015 film *The Danish Girl*, in which she is portrayed by English actor Eddie Redmayne.

1969 *Gay*, the first weekly gay magazine, is issued in the United States.

1969 The Stonewall Riots, a series of spontaneous demonstrations by members of the gay community protesting a police raid on the Stonewall Inn in New York City. This event is often considered the beginning of the modern gay liberation movement and the modern fight for LGBTQIA+ rights in the United States.

1970 Transgender actress Holly Woodlawn is immortalized by gay artist Andy Warhol in the film *Trash*. She is later the inspiration for Lou Reed's song, "Walk On The Wild Side." David Bowie releases the album *Man Who Sold The World*, an image of him in a dress appearing on the front cover.

1972 Australian soap opera *Number 96* introduces its first openly gay character. Also, *That Certain Summer* becomes the first gay themed American show to win an Emmy Award.

1973 Activist, lesbian, and poet Audre Lorde publishes *From a Land Where Other People Live*, a National Book Award finalist.

Chris Bartlett

1974 *The New York Times* publishes "Homosexuals in New York: The Gay World."

1975 Tim Curry and Richard O'Brien release *The Rocky Horror Picture Show*, a highly controversial film at the time addressing gender, cross-dressing, and gay and bisexual relationships.

1976 World famous singer Sir Elton John publicly identifies as bisexual in an interview with *Rolling Stone* magazine. Also, the first issue of lesbian magazine *Sinister Wisdom* is published.

1977 Openly gay political candidate and activist Harvey Milk wins a seat on the San Francisco Board of Supervisors. He is murdered the following year.

1980s The New Romantic movement arrives in the United Kingdom with gender non-conforming acts like Boy George, Dead or Alive and The Cure taking center stage.
CBS broadcasts the documentary *Gay Power, Gay Politics*.

1983 Openly gay award winning actor and playwright Harvey Fierstein writes and stars in the hit Broadway play *Torch Song Trilogy*. This is followed by the book *La Cage aux Folles*. Both works pay tribute to gay culture and community.

1984 Openly gay athlete Greg Louganis

What Does "Queer" Mean Anyway?

wins four gold medals in the Olympics. *NOW*, the popular music label, sponsors a conference on lesbian rights. Queen releases the music video for "I want to break free," in which the band members cross- dress as women.

1988 Sir Elton John comes out as gay to *Rolling Stone* magazine. Famous British actor and future *The Lord of the Rings* star Sir Ian McKellen also comes out the same year.

1991 Television show *The Golden Girls* airs an episode in support of gay marriage. Meanwhile, Freddy Mercury announces he has AIDS, leading to further awareness of the disease; he dies the next day.

1992 British drag queen act Lily Savage (portrayed by Paul O'Grady) begins making television and radio appearances.

1993 Film Director Jonathan Demme pairs up with actor Tom Hanks to release *Philidelphia*, a film that directly tackles prejudice and opens up the AIDS debate.

1993 RuPaul, a drag queen, actor, model, and author, records the album *Supermodel to the World*, achieving international acclaim, success, and fame.

1997 Comedian and actress Ellen DeGeneres announces she is a lesbian live on the *Oprah Winfrey Show*.

1998 *Gay Parent* magazine begins publishing online.

1999 Singer George Michael comes out as gay in an interview with *The Advocate*. Prior to this he had claimed to be bisexual and performed a number of concerts for AIDS awareness following the death of his partner to the disease.

2002 The "Sunday Styles" section of *The New York Times* begins publishing congratulatory reports of same-sex civil ceremonies.

2004 TV series *The L Word* is piloted, a fresh series about lesbian relationships; it goes on for six seasons.

2013 Disney releases the animated film *Frozen*, featuring their first-ever gay character (Oaken) who waves to his husband and children midway through the film. Albeit this was done with plausible deniability of the character's orientation, it is obvious that the creators are winking at certain audience members.

2015 Caitlyn Jenner, formerly known as Bruce Jenner and a retired gold medal-winning decathlete, reveals her identity as a trans woman and goes on to star in the reality television series *I am Cait*, which focuses on her gender transition.

What Does "Queer" Mean Anyway?

2015 Actor and son of Will Smith, Jaden Smith, states he is gender fluid and begins gender-neutral fashion modeling.

Popular culture and the power of celebrity will inevitably continue to assist in the understanding and acceptance of gender fluidity and LGBTQIA+ culture. From mainstream music and theater to hard-hitting literature and activist magazines, there are many ways in which the general public can be inspired, challenged, and educated in what it means to exist outside of the traditional gender boundaries.

Conclusion

Many people are directly or indirectly affected by the recent successes of the gay rights movements, gender equality issues, and gender non-conformity and transgender breakthroughs. The amazing development of new words and phrases allows for the English language to flexibly adapt to the evolving concepts of gender and sexuality. It can, of course, sometimes be difficult to understand these complexities without personal examples to highlight them, and hopefully this book has illustrated just how diverse the nature of gender can be.

There are several key elements to take away from this book. These are:

1. Gender and sexuality are not the same thing, but can sometimes interlink or overlap depending on individual circumstances.
2. LGBTQIA+ is an acronym that is designed to group together lesbian, gay, bisexual, transgender, intersex, queer, and asexual people, but this

What Does "Queer" Mean Anyway?

acronym can be displayed in other ways to involve other identities on the spectrum.

3. There are several gender-neutral pronouns that are often more appropriate when describing someone whose gender is nonconforming or nonbinary, but no standardization of pronoun use.
4. There are many words that are no longer acceptable to use when talking to or about an LGBTQIA+ person, and many words that are preferred.
5. Relationships can be complicated with a transgender person, but each couple is different and support is available.
6. Popular culture has played an important part in LGBTQIA+ history and present day movements.
7. Transgenderism and intersex are two different things, and affect people in entirely different ways.
8. Why some people are transgender and some are not is unknown. In the past it has been treated as a medical condition that needed to be cured — but then again, so has left-handedness.

9. Many LGBTQIA+ people still suffer discrimination and prejudice, and often this can be heightened depending on their geographical location.

10. Gender is a social construct that will always be evolving and changing.

As a final thought, it is important to keep an open mind when it comes to sexuality and gender. Every human is different and unique, with individual biology, psychology, and feelings. Each story is different, and there is no one-size- fits-all approach to identity. By using the correct language and understanding the inner workings of the LGBTQIA+ and gender spectrum, we can work towards a more harmonious society in which all humans are regarded as valued and equal.

What Does "Queer" Mean Anyway?

To My Friends in the LGBTQIA+ Community

First of all: Thank you for reading and purchasing this book.

Second of all: If this book failed to adequately explain your identity or the identity of someone you care about, you have my apologies. The purpose of this book was to introduce concepts and identities from within the LGBTQIA+ spectrum to people who are unfamiliar with them and perhaps even uncomfortable with these ideas. To do so effectively, there were times I had to make compromises between comprehensive explanations and accessible ones.

One of the wonderful things about e-books and print-to-order books is that it is easy to update the material. If there is a concept or explanation which I left out, explained inadequately, or even mangled beyond recognition, then I encourage you to e-mail me at chris@thequickanddirtyguide.com and give me the opportunity to update the text.

When I started this project I did not conceive of the stress and emotional energy it would require. When I began researching and speaking with friends and acquaintances whose identities I was attempting to explain, I was overwhelmed by the levels of support I received and passion that I witnessed. There were moments during this book's production in which I, as a heterosexual, cisgendered male, felt wholly unequal to the task, but the encouragement I received from community members of various identities convinced me to press forward.

Third of all: I wish to thank those (of all identities) who helped me produce this book, including my editors, friends, family members, pre-readers, and anyone else who allowed me the opportunity share my concerns and anxieties regarding producing a text of this nature.

Bibliography

American Psychological Association (2015) *Answers to Your Questions About Transgender People, Gender Identity and Gender Expression*. Online. Available at http://www.apa.org/topics/lgbt/transgender.aspx. Accessed 26 May 2016.

CBC/Radio-Canada (2016) *Transforming Gender*: "Timeline: Transgender Through History." Online. Available at http://www.cbc.ca/doczone/features/timeline-transgender-through-history. Accessed 27 May 2016.

Chavez, Cesar (2010) *GeneQ*. Berkeley.Edu.. Available at https://www.ocf.berkeley.edu/~geneq/docs/info Sheets/Queer.pdf. Accessed 25 May 2016.

Coleman, Eli et al (2012) *Standards of Care for the Health of Transsexual, Transgender, and Gender-Nonconforming People* (pdf). The World Professional Association for Transgender Health. Online. Available at http://www.wpath.org/uploaded_files/140/files/Standards%20of%20Care,%20V7%20Full%20Boo k.pdf. Accessed 25 May 2016.

Conway, L. (2003) "What Causes Transsexualism?" Online. Available at http://ai.eecs.umich.edu/people/conway/TS/TSc auses.html. Accessed 25 May 2016.

Garofalo, R. (2012) "Understanding Gender Nonconformity in Childhood and Adolescence" (pdf). Children's Hospital Of Chicago. Online.
Available at https://www.aap.org/en-us/Documents/solgbt_webinar_transition_garof alo.pdf. Accessed 27 May 2016.

Gates, G. (2011) "How Many People Are Lesbian, Gay, Bisexual, and Transgender?" p.1. The Williams Institute. Online. Available at http://williamsinstitute.law.ucla.edu/wp-content/uploads/Gates-How-Many-People-LGBT- Apr-2011.pdf. Accessed 30 May 2016.

Hamzelou, J. (2011) "Transsexual Differences Caught on Brain Scan." New Scientist. Online. Available at https://www.newscientist.com/article/dn20032-transsexual-differences-caught-on-brain-scan/. Accessed 25 May 2016.

Kaneshiro, N. K., (2015) "Intersex." Medline Plus. (Online) available at

What Does "Queer" Mean Anyway?

https://www.nlm.nih.gov/medlineplus/ency/arti cle/001669.htm. Accessed 26 May 2016.

Lutz, T. (2001) *Crying: A Natural and Cultural History of Tears*. W. W. Norton & Company.

Mchugh, P. (2014) "Transgender Surgery Isn't The Solution." *The Wall Street Journal*. Online. Available at http://www.wsj.com/articles/paul-mchugh-transgender-surgery-isnt-the-solution- 1402615120. Accessed 30 May 2016.

Meier, Colton S. et al, (2013) *Romantic Relationships of Female-to-Male Trans Men: A Descriptive Study*. University of Houston.

International Journal Of Transgenderism. Online. Available at http://uh.edu/class/psychology/clinical-psych/research/dpl/ files/publications/Meier- Sharp-Michonski-Babcock-and- Fitzgerald 2013.pdf. Accessed 30 May 2016.

Meyerowitz, J. (2002) *How Sex Changed: A History of Transsexuality in the United States* p. 32. Harvard University Press.

NHS Choices (2016) "Gender Dysphoria." Online. Available at http://www.nhs.uk/conditions/gender-dysphoria/Pages/Introduction.aspx. Accessed 26 May 2016.

ProCon.org (2014) "Gay Marriage Timeline." Online. Available at http://gaymarriage.procon.org/view.timeline.ph p?timelineID=000030#1970-1999. Accessed 28 May 2016.

Wolchover, N. (2012) "Why Is Pink For Girls and Blue For Boys?" LiveScience. Online. Available at http://www.livescience.com/22037-pink-girls- blue-boys.html. Accessed 30 May 2016.

Women's Resource Centre (2016) "Fact Sheet: Transgender, Transsexual and Intersex" p. 1. University Of Colorado Denver. Online. Available at http://www.ucdenver.edu/life/services/studentli fe/WRC/Fact%20Sheets/trans.pdf. Accessed 26 May 2016.

I Need Your Help

Thank you so much for reading this book. When I started my self-publishing journey I never imagined the satisfaction that could come from someone reading something into which I put so much time. As this is a self-published book I do not have the resources of a major publisher for marketing or promotion and am reliant upon the appreciation and goodwill of my readers. If this book brought value to you and you believe it could be valuable to another then I ask that you leave a review at this product's Amazon webpage. You can also purchase a copy of this text in ebook or audiobook forms there.

Stay informed about my next project!

Another way that you could help out is by signing up for the *Quick and Dirty Newsletter*. You'll receive a free copy of another *Quick and Dirty Guide* and receive updates on forthcoming books, including my follow up to this book The Quick and Dirty Guide to the Five Biggest Events in American LGBT History. Go to www.thequickanddirtyguide.com to sign up!

Made in the USA
San Bernardino, CA
29 January 2018